An Hachette UK Company
www.hachette.co.uk

First published in Great Britain
in 2021 by Aster, an imprint of Octopus
Publishing Group Ltd
Carmelite House,
50 Victoria Embankment,
London EC4Y 0DZ
www.octopusbooks.co.uk

ISBN 978 1 78325 435 4

A CIP catalogue record for this book is
available from the British Library.

Printed and bound in China

10 9 8 7 6 5 4 3 2 1

Consultant Publisher: Kate Adams
Art Director: Yasia Williams-Leedham
Illustrators: SpaceFrog Designs
Senior Editor: Alex Stetter
Copy Editor: Caroline West
Production Manager: Allison Gonsalves

morning meditations

To focus the mind and wake up
your energy for the day ahead

aster

Danielle North

Contents

Introduction
The beauty of mornings

We are often in a hurry in the morning. Trying to get somewhere as the new day dawns. It seems so habitual to jump into action as soon as we get out of bed, so necessary almost to get up, grab a coffee and get going.

Yet there is an energy in the early hours of the day that is beautifully silent, still and peaceful. A time before the dawn has fully broken, when the birds have not yet started singing, when the connection to spirit (and therefore to yourself) is available more fully than at any other time of day. This space between the end of the night and the beginning of the day is a place suited to silence. It is a time of meditation and of the realms of the dreamworld, and a perfect place to connect more deeply with yourself as the day begins. Holding this still and sacred space is the beauty of mornings.

It's not always possible when you are juggling a lot of priorities, but what if the stillness could support the juggle? Keep it simple to start with and set your alarm ten minutes early, so you can enjoy your morning tea in silence. Or perhaps turn off the alarm and the radio at weekends and experience silence as you wake up naturally to start your day.

When we wake up in the morning, there is a subtle space between waking and reality. That space holds an emptiness before the thoughts begin to crowd the mind, and how welcome those thoughts are will depend on how you feel and what is going on in your life.

You might wake from a dream and feel as if that dream state is your waking state – and you emerge into your day feeling deliciously cosy or deeply grateful. Or perhaps you wake feeling disorientated, with a jolt, experiencing the emotions you had while you were dreaming, gasping for breath, or with tears rolling down your cheeks, or your heart tight with anxiety. For some people, going to bed doesn't mean falling asleep or staying asleep, so you may already have been awake long before dawn. However you start your day, there is an opportunity to treat that space as special and sacred by using morning rituals.

The following suggestions are just that – suggestions. These rituals are not a list of requirements that you have to incorporate into your morning, but food for thought and perhaps inspiration for you to deepen your relationship with yourself, become grounded and have greater clarity, focus and direction.

By their very nature, rituals work best when practised regularly over time. When we do that, the ritual eventually becomes so natural, so habitual, that life without it would seem strange. But there is a period of time before that happens when the practice might feel challenging or too time-consuming, and it's sticking to it during these times that eventually leads to a breakthrough. To get started, I suggest you choose one or two rituals and weave them into your morning routine for six months, to discover what happens.

As you prepare to go on the journey these pages offer, I want to share a final note to remind you that day and night are connected. Light does not exist without the dark. How you end your day and how you begin your day are symbiotic and functioning with them as part of a whole will bring positive benefits to your overall experience of living.

May your beautiful soul always shine brightly.

Mountains of love,
Danielle x

On waking

Are your mornings a chaotic mix of dogs, children and packed lunches? Do you hit the snooze button and squeeze every last delicious second out of being under the covers? Or are your senses immediately blasted by the news, emails and social media? Whatever your morning looks like, you may think it's impossible to carve out any extra time for yourself. If that's the case, start small and start as soon as you wake up. Here are three quick health practices you can build into your mornings.

1. Clean your teeth and scrape your tongue. Overnight your body has been working brilliantly to detox your system, and some of the results of that process are now in your mouth in the form of bacteria. So, as soon as you get up, before you consume anything, brush your teeth and use a tongue scraper to clean your tongue – it only takes a few extra seconds.

2. While you're there, take a few seconds to look in the mirror. Look beyond your face and into your eyes, letting yourself see deep within. Place your hand on your heart, say your name and then something positive to start your day. If you're unsure what to say, then simply say, 'I love you.'

3. Drink water before your morning coffee. Coffee will dehydrate your cells and, as you've not had any fluids for a number of hours, that's a quick route to a tension headache. So, drink a large glass of warm (not iced) water when you wake up.

Write your dreams

Every dream is a private and individual communication. How you dream and what your dreams are communicating are unique to you. Dreams constitute some of the most personal and precious guidance we can receive in our lives. If you are seeking clarity and direction in your life, or perhaps greater meaning and purpose, or you are working through a difficulty or challenge, a dream is a place you can trust for guidance.

However, dreams are not easy to understand. Our dreamworld is different to our waking world, and the way in which we construct ideas and thoughts in a logical, often linear, way when we are awake is not how things function when we are asleep. Instead, the dream reveals itself in symbols and patterns, time takes on an entirely different meaning, and sometimes when we wake our recollection of the dream is hazy, vague or non-existent.

Dreams are sometimes described as being good or bad, but because the dreamworld works in symbols, what is deemed bad in the waking world may be positive in the dream. For instance, in a dream, killing another person can symbolize growth and development, as you have learned to be less vulnerable to attack and are more able to defend yourself.

Remember, any interpretation must be linked to you and the context of your life. For this reason, looking up the meaning of your dream online is utterly pointless. Your dream is for *you* in the context of *your* life, and the practice involves learning to understand the meaning of the symbols for yourself.

Even if a dream isn't easy to understand, we should always assume that it is relevant and has meaning. Your dreams are doing more than simply processing and filing away previous experiences. Your dreams are revealing new, and as yet unseen, information to you, and it is this that makes taking the time to understand them particularly meaningful.

If you don't remember your dreams, it doesn't mean you're not dreaming. If you experiment with other practices for a few months, you may notice that your dream recall returns, or you may wish to give yourself time in the mornings to reflect on your dreams, even if you can't consciously recall them. Over time this may change. As you might have experienced, many dreams drift away as soon as conscious thought returns.

Allowing yourself time to wake up naturally and slowly can provide you with the space you need to recall your dreams. It can help to write them down immediately, so keep a dream journal by your bed. Make a note of the date and then write down the dream exactly as it happened, no matter how strange it may seem. Make notes of the key symbols and what the dream means to you, particularly in the context of your life as it is. Over time, the dream forms a story, often with recurring themes and connected chapters. The dream is one of the most powerful sources of guidance you can receive. Treasure this and put it to good use.

See the sky before a screen

Many of us check our smartphone within minutes of waking up. Changing this habit is quite easy and has plenty of positive health benefits. Creating a sacred start to your day begins the night before, by turning off your smartphone entirely (not just putting it on 'airplane mode') and charging it overnight in a room other than your bedroom. If you need an alarm to wake you up, then invest in an alarm clock – they really do work!

You can also set your router to turn your Wi-Fi off from a certain time at night until a certain time in the morning. This will make it less tempting to log in when you first wake up.

Before you switch on any devices in the morning, take a moment to look at the sky. This may be through a window or your open front door, by standing in the garden (barefoot is even more grounding) or going for a walk. However you do this, take a few deep breaths (see *Simple Morning Breathwork*, on the next page, for some tips), look up at the sky and acknowledge the new day by saying:

I am alive,
On this new day.
In this moment,
I am thankful.

Now is a good time to set an intention for your day ahead. See *The Power of Intention*, on page 29, for tips on how to do this.

Simple morning breathwork

Many people breathe backwards, which means they inhale by pulling in the belly. When we draw the belly in on the inhale, there is less space for the breath rather than more. This is called Paradoxical Breathing (also known as the 'Fear Breath'). People who are often anxious or smoke frequently tend to have this breathing pattern, or they learn it because they have suffered a shock or are terrified by something in life.

Even if you don't experience Paradoxical Breathing, most of us have shallow chest breathing, which means our brains, blood and other vital organs don't get enough oxygen. These breathing patterns can be easily changed by practising the three simple breathwork techniques described opposite. They take just a couple of minutes and can be built into your morning routine.

Choose one breathwork technique to practise at a time rather than trying them all in a row. Sit comfortably, with your spine straight, shoulders down and collarbones open. Gaze directly out in front of you. Sitting correctly is important to ensure that your body is supported, so you can breathe correctly.

✳ *Water breathing* is a breath in through the nose and out through the mouth. Use this breath for slowing down and centring. Water breathing connects us with our emotions so that we can experience our deeper self.

Place one hand on your chest and the other on your belly. Inhale deeply through the nose, down into your belly, and exhale through an open mouth. Repeat five times. Practise for longer as your lungs strengthen.

✳ *Fire breathing* is a breath in through the mouth and out through the nose. It is good for creating energy and heat, so use this breath if you are feeling low or demotivated. (Note: this is not same as the Yogic Breath of Fire, which is a rapid nostril-breathing technique.)

Place one hand on your chest and the other on your belly. Inhale deeply through an open mouth for five seconds. Hold for one or two seconds. Exhale through an open mouth for five seconds. Repeat five times. Practise for longer as your lungs strengthen.

✳ *Extended breathing* is a breathing technique in which the exhale is longer than the inhale. This is good for resetting the central nervous system when you are feeling anxious or overwhelmed.

Place one hand on your chest and the other on your belly. Inhale deeply through your nose for a count of four, hold for a count of four, and then exhale through an open mouth for a count of eight. Repeat five times. Practise for a little longer if you are still feeling anxious.

Qigong to cultivate energy

Qigong is an ancient system of movement and breathing which is designed to cultivate and harmonize the body's natural energy or qi. In China, qi is known as life force, a universal energy that is in and around us all. *Qi* roughly translates as 'life energy' and it is what makes up and binds together all things in the universe. You may also see qi spelled c'hi, chi, ki or khi.

Qigong is a standing practice and may be described as a moving meditation, using the breath and movement, movement and breath, so that you can be in the present moment. Qigong also has the added benefits of releasing endorphins and reducing stress. In the warmer months, qigong can also be practised outside in nature for further benefits.

Start by training for ten minutes a day, three times a week. There are many wonderful, free qigong resources available on YouTube, with trained teachers who can guide you through the sessions.

Energizing essential oils

If you have time in the morning, then putting on a diffuser with an energizing essential oil is a natural way to enhance your mood and stimulate your senses. There is a huge variety of essential oils to choose from. Here are suggestions for three essential oils you can use in the mornings, each of which has different benefits:

❋ *Bergamot:* The sunny citrus scent of this oil is excellent for raising a low mood.

❋ *Peppermint:* A perfect essential oil to use if you have a big day ahead as it stimulates clear thinking.

❋ *Basil:* This oil is ideal if you are feeling burned-out and need a boost because it rejuvenates a weary body.

Lighting a candle is a simple ritual with which to start your day, and some good-quality candles also contain mood-enhancing essential oils, so you get double the benefit. Always remember to blow candles out before you leave the house.

If you don't have time for these rituals, then look for natural soaps, shower gels, scrubs and shampoos containing scents such as grapefruit, ginger, lemon, black pepper, wild orange or lime, and gift yourself a morning lift in the shower.

Reflections through tea

'Tea connects us to nature.
We haven't lost our connection to nature,
We've lost the feeling of our connection to nature.'

(Wu De, Chajin and Zen monk, Global Tea Hut)

Tea is a worldwide ritual, from the sweet, steaming-hot, long-poured mint tea in Morocco to the institution that is afternoon tea in the UK. Tea was introduced to the world by the Chinese, with *Cha Dao* referring to the art of tea-making. *Cha Dao* has close links with Daoism and the Chinese philosophies of balance, harmony, fulfilment and enjoyment.

Thousands of years ago, Buddhist monks discovered that drinking tea allowed them to maintain a state of 'mindful alertness' during long periods of meditation; this is because, unlike coffee, tea contains a unique combination of caffeine and a compound called L-theanine. This rare amino acid creates alpha waves, which lead to a state of relaxed alertness. L-theanine also moderates the caffeine in tea, so that you can be focused and alert, while also feeling calm and relaxed.

Leaves in a bowl tea ceremony

A tea practice simply involves heat, water and tea. If you would like to introduce *Cha Dao* into your life, you can practise the Leaves in a Bowl Tea Ceremony below, which is taught by Wu De at the Global Tea Hut. Wu De advises that you should begin your tea practice with a trial of drinking at least three bowls of tea every day for a week: 'Put the tea in the bowl, add water and don't worry about the method at this stage. The only rule is no multi-tasking – no phone, no music, no talking.'

To practise this meditative tea ceremony, you will need:

* Sustainably produced, organic, loose-leaf tea (white, green, red, oolong, black or Pu-erh)
* Water (spring water, if possible)
* Kettle
* Bowl
* Quiet, clear space (to drink the tea)

For the ritual, complete each of the steps mindfully:

Step 1 Put some of the loose-leaf tea in the bowl.

Step 2 Pour hot water over the tea leaves.

Step 3 Sit in a comfortable cross-legged position.

Step 4 Hold the bowl in both hands. Drink three or more bowls of tea in silence (using the same leaves for each bowl).

Repeat these steps for a week – you will need to set aside at least 20 minutes a day for this ritual.

Reflections through tea

Matcha ritual

'When you hear the splash
Of the water drops that fall
Into the stone bowl,
You will feel that all the dust
Of your mind is washed away.'
(Sen no Rikyu, Grand Tea Master, 1522–1591)

In Japan, tea huts have been serving matcha tea for centuries in traditional ceremonies called *Chadō*, which translates as 'The Way of Tea'. Matcha tea is a fine powder that is ground from the leaves of the green tea plant. The plants are covered and grown in the shade for three to four weeks before they are harvested, which has the effect of producing more caffeine and L-theanine. Rich in antioxidants, matcha tea is essentially a superfood!

To make matcha tea, you'll need some simple equipment and a few accessories:

* Matcha tea bowl and chasen, which is a small bamboo whisk (both essential)
* Chashaku, a traditional bamboo tea scoop used in tea ceremonies, and a small sifter to create a smooth, foamy bowl of tea (both optional)

* Matcha tea, which is available in different grades and quality, meaning that each matcha has different notes and unique flavours (ceremonial-grade matcha is the highest quality, but you can explore your personal preference)
* Kettle for hot water (ensure the water is not boiling, but around 75–80°C/167–176°F – you may wish to use a thermometer to check the temperature)
* Quiet, clear space (to drink the tea)

For the ritual, complete each of the steps mindfully:

Step 1 Heat the bowl by adding some boiling water. Put the whisk in the bowl for a minute or two to soften the bamboo.

Step 2 Pour away the water and dry the bowl thoroughly.

Step 3 Sift two or three scoops of matcha into your bowl (about 3g), adjusting the amount according to the size of your bowl and taste preferences.

Step 4 Add 100ml (3fl oz) of cooled boiled water (per 2–3g of tea) to the bowl. Make sure you don't scald the delicate tea by using water cooled to a temperature of about 75–80°C (167–176°F).

Step 5 Begin whisking the matcha, starting slowly and then gradually increasing the speed. Whisk in a 'W'-motion, close to the surface of the tea, until you have a frothy top. Be vigorous!

Step 6 Sit quietly and enjoy.

Notes on meditation

Meditation is a way of cultivating compassion, inner peace and wisdom. You do this by learning to focus your awareness, which, over time, allows you to observe your experience without judgement. You can practise meditation alone or join a group. It can take practice and patience to learn how to meditate, but it's really worth it!

Why meditate?

Meditation marks a special moment in your day when you can pause and be with yourself and your own experience for a short while. Meditation increases concentration, deepens self-awareness and reduces stress. Over time, you may find that meditation also improves your sleep, enhances your creativity and even improves the quality of your relationships.

How to meditate

To begin with, meditation might feel uncomfortable: your body may feel tight and your mind like a runaway train. The whole experience can quickly lead to you feeling frustrated, and so you give up. It's normal to go through these experiences. Here are five simple ways to get started with meditation, even if it has been difficult for you in the past.

1. Set your space

Both the body and mind like routine, so having a set place you go to each day to meditate enables you to settle into your meditation. You might want to place a candle, some incense or a crystal in the place where you meditate. A blanket can also be useful so you don't become cold during your meditation.

2. Set your time

As before, setting a regular time of day when you meditate helps encourage your body and mind into the practice. When you wake up is an ideal time, before your mind becomes too distracted by the day. Avoid stimulants like coffee or nicotine before you meditate. However, see *Reflections Through Tea*, pages 20–23, for tips on how some teas can help you to concentrate and stay alert.

To start with, the length of time you meditate for is less important than getting into the routine of sitting in your space. When you meditate, it isn't advisable to end your practice with an alarm, as this will jolt you out of a peaceful place in quite a harsh way. If you have time, let yourself sit for as long as you are able; if you are pressed for time, then use the counting technique outlined on page 30 to develop your practice. Morning is the perfect time to meditate and setting yourself a specific time when you go to your meditation space each day creates a rhythm that will ultimately support your practice.

3. Set your body

Sitting comfortably makes meditation easier, as you're not being distracted by niggles in the body. I suggest that you support your back for extra comfort. A meditation seat or cushion can really help because they allow your hips to be raised and your back supported. If you are sitting in an easy chair, make sure your hands are empty, your back feels supported (perhaps put a couple of cushions behind you), and both feet are on the floor. When you are ready to begin, tilt your chin slightly to your chest, lower your gaze or close your eyes and let your tongue gently rest on the roof of your mouth.

4. Set your intention

This is an optional step, but you may want to set an intention for your practice (see *The Power of Intention*, on page 29). For instance, to be open, or kind to yourself or loving to others. Alternatively, you could chant the sound of 'Om' three times.

5. Set your breath

When you meditate, your focus will be on your breathing. Begin by taking three conscious breaths, a deep inhale in through the nose, down into your belly and out through the mouth, as if you are blowing out a candle. I like to inhale an essential oil at this stage. I roll a pre-blended aroma in the palm of my hands, and then cup my hands over my face as I inhale. This helps anchor the body and mind into the practice. Then, let your breathing become normal and focus on the breath as it enters and exits your body. Simply follow your breath. If at any time your mind gets busy or you drift off, simply come back to your breath.

That's it, you are meditating!

When you have finished, you can complete with the sound of 'Om' again or by bringing your hands together in prayer at your heart centre and acknowledging yourself for your practice.

Finally, like anything new, meditation takes time to learn, so keep a beginner's mindset and let the practice teach you as you grow and develop over time.

Morning affirmations

Our thoughts can send powerful messages into the world and into our own being. Given the power of words and language, either spoken or thought, have you ever considered what you say to yourself? How kind and loving are you towards yourself? If you don't want to develop a meditation practice at this time, that's OK. You could simply practise being kind in your thoughts towards yourself. The affirmations below can be said silently to yourself, spoken aloud (looking into your eyes in a mirror if you want to go deeper) or even sung.

For grounding yourself, choose an affirmation you feel drawn to and repeat it to yourself in the morning and throughout the day:

I am here   *I am loved*
I am me   *I am centred*
I am whole   *I am balanced*
I am safe   *I am peaceful*
I am strong   *I am grounded*

For expansion, choose one of the affirmations below or create your own using a similar structure of 'I am...'

I am returning to my true nature/essence
I am opening my heart to love
I am radiating joy and gratitude

The power of intention

Wherever we put our thoughts, our energy follows, so it's important to be mindful of the dialogue we have with ourselves and of the thoughts we send out into the world. All actions have an intention behind them; sometimes it is conscious and at other times it is unconscious. We can use the power of our thoughts in a positive way through conscious intention setting. When we set positive intentions, it's like dropping a stone in a lake: it cannot help but make ripples.

Intentions can be set in the morning as part of your meditation practice, or you can simply sit quietly with yourself for a couple of minutes. An intention is not a demand or expectation; it is a purposeful awareness of how you want to experience something, which usually includes yourself. Intentions are different to goals, because goals have an end point or a destination to aim for, while intentions are based on your day-to-day experience. Intentions can, for example, be set to focus on how you want to feel, how you want to act and behave in certain situations, or how you want to treat others.

Intentions are always set within a positive framework, not from a place of lack or something being missing. So, rather than setting an intention that says, 'I don't want to be afraid', you could say, 'I am feeling strong and confident in every way, every day.' Intentions have love and kindness running through them, which is what makes intention setting such a powerful way to start your day.

Developing your practice

Use the following five tips to develop your meditation practice and so gain more from it.

Aroma
Use scent to anchor your practice, choosing an incense, such as sandalwood or frankincense, or an essential-oil blend. Essential-oil blends can be made at home, or you can buy a pre-mixed meditation oil in a rollerball. Simply roll the oil into the palm of your left hand. Rub your hands together anti-clockwise to release the aroma, cup your palms over your face, and then inhale and exhale long and slow three times. If you wish, you can then place your hands on any part of your body that needs some love and care.

Music
People often think they have to meditate in silence, but if you prefer to have some background music on, that can be very helpful, particularly if you use the same music each time. This repetition allows your body and mind to become anchored, understanding that this is now a meditative moment. If you are unsure what to listen to, try Jane Winther for grounding chants or Beautiful Chorus for uplifting mantras.

Counting
The mind loves a distraction and counting during meditation does just that. Providing a structure for your meditation in this way means you don't need to focus on the length of time you're meditating for. There are different techniques for focusing your

attention on counting during meditation, one of which is to count the number of breaths. One breath is an inhale and an exhale. One cycle is ten breaths. Start with one or two cycles and build up to ten. If you lose count, go back to the beginning.

Body tuners

If you want to turbo-charge your meditation practice, invest in a set of good-quality body tuners, which are C and G tuning forks. When tapped together, the forks create a 'perfect fifth', which represents universal balance and harmony. When you listen to these two tones simultaneously, the body unites them to make one tone internally, and a gateway to healing and accessing higher consciousness is opened.

Hold one tuning fork in your left hand and the other in your right hand. Tap the tuning forks together at the start of the meditation and hold the forks close to your ears (right hand to right ear, left hand to left ear) until the sound dissipates. You can ring them again at the end of the meditation. Alternatively, hold one fork in each hand, tap them together and, holding them close to each other, draw the forks around the outer edges of your body. This can be done at the beginning and/or end of the meditation to bring your nervous system into balance.

Nature

At the weekend, or on holiday, it can be very special to deepen your experience by going into nature to meditate. You can sit on a rock by a river, take a crystal and hold it as you nestle into the trunk of a tree, find a spot to sit deep in a forest or woodland, get fresh perspectives at sunrise on top of a hill, or meditate to the rhythmical sounds of the ocean waves lapping the shore.

* Morning meditations

The Meditations

For each of the meditations in this chapter, begin by setting your space: light a candle or some incense and choose your music, if you want this. Have a blanket or wrap close by to keep you warm if necessary. Most of the meditations are performed seated, so set your body by sitting in a comfortable position with your spine straight, but not stiff. If you are sitting on a cushion, cross your legs; if you are sitting in a chair, place both feet flat on the floor.

Rest your hands in your lap or on your knees. If you are using an essential oil, roll this onto the palm of your left hand. Rub your hands together in an anti-clockwise direction, then cup your palms over your face and inhale long and slow three times. If you aren't using an aroma, that's OK; simply inhale and exhale long and slow three times.

Take a moment to set a positive intention for today's meditation. Lower your gaze and tip your chin to your chest, turning your attention inwards as you gently bring your eyelids together and focus on your breath entering and leaving your body. As you focus on your breath, set your intention for your meditation or your day (or both).

Awakening

✳ You are all wrapped up in a cosy blanket, feeling comfortable, safe and secure, like a caterpillar contained in a chrysalis. If you want to wrap your arms around your body for extra comfort, now is a good time to do so. Focus on your breathing, letting it be steady and even, deep and slow, for ten breaths. With each breath repeat the mantra: 'I am safe right here, right now.'

Begin by letting your mind wander back to the experiences in your life that have brought you to this moment. Occasions when you might have felt vulnerable, challenged or exposed. Choose one of those times and let yourself recall the parts of you that felt fragile or delicate during that experience.

Let go of the need to be strong in this moment.

Allow yourself to feel the fragility, knowing that you are safe right here in this moment, right now.

As you connect to the more delicate parts of you, take a breath and begin to see the strength in the delicacy. Like the veins on the underside of a butterfly's wings, how does this delicacy support you? Where is there strength in the fragility? How does this strength serve you today? Thank yourself for being who you are. Thank the others involved for their part in your growth in this lifetime. Thank life for supporting you.

Take another breath deep into your tummy and exhale long and slow out through your mouth, letting your arms or blanket loosen around you. Allow the protective chrysalis to slip slowly away as you emerge like a butterfly, knowing that the lessons live on within you and make you stronger and even more radiant. Let your beauty shine from the inside out and fly free knowing all is well.

Affirmation: 'I am safe right here, right now.'

Just for today

❋ Begin this meditation by focusing on your mind. Become aware of the thoughts in your mind and, just for today, let them be. Thoughts will come and go, swirling like leaves in the breeze; just for today, let them simply be the movements of the mind.

Thoughts are constantly in motion; it's what the mind does. Whether your mind feels chaotic or peaceful, let the movement of the mind be the movement of the mind. Just for today. If your mind is highly active, observe it being active. Allow it to be active and observe the movement of the mind simply being the movement of the mind.

Just for today, observe that you are not your mind. You have a mind, but you are not your mind.

Now become aware of your emotions. What are you feeling? Simply observe and notice your emotions. Where do you feel these emotional energies? Do your emotions have colour or density or temperature? Are your emotions highly active or are they peaceful? Emotions want to move; it is what emotions do. In this moment, just for today, simply notice that your emotions are energy. Observe your emotions changing moment by moment and allow them to move and flow. Just for today, observe that you are not your emotions. You have emotions, but you are not your emotions.

Be aware that you have a mind and emotions, but you are not your mind and emotions. That whatever your mind and emotions are doing, you can still remain peaceful in your being. Even if the mind and emotions are highly active, you can continue to be peaceful.

As you sit in this peaceful place of observation, letting your mind and emotions move and change and flow, ask the following questions:

Just for today can you be easy on yourself?
Not forever, just for today.

Breathe it in.
Let it out.
Breathe it in.
Let it go.

Just for today can you be easy on others?
Not forever, just for today.

Breathe it in.
Let it out.
Breathe it in.
Let it go.

Just for today can you open your heart to yourself?
Not forever, just for today.

Breathe it in.
Let it out.
Breathe it in.
Let it go.

Just for today can you open your heart to others?
Not forever, just for today.

Breathe it in.
Let it out.
Breathe it in.
Let it go.

*Just for today can you be true to
yourself?*
Not forever, just for today.

Breathe it in.
Let it out.
Breathe it in.
Let it go.

*Just for today can you be true to
others?*
Not forever, just for today.

Breathe it in.
Let it out.
Breathe it in.
Let it go.

*Just for today can you be with life
exactly as it is?*
Not forever, just for today.

Breathe it in.
Let it out.

Breathe it in.
Let it go.

Return to your natural breathing now, letting your mind and emotions flow freely, ever moving, ever changing. Take a deep inhale and an easy exhale. When you are ready, return to the room, safe in the knowledge that we can live our lives, moment by moment, day by day.

Affirmation: 'I can be with life just as it is.'

Radiant light

✳ If you would like to begin with an intention, sit quietly and say to yourself: 'I am open to receive divine light.' For this meditation, place both hands on the centre of your torso, just above your belly button, and, as you inhale, count slowly to three, 1, 2, 3, contracting your belly. As you exhale, count slowly to three, 1, 2, 3, expanding your belly. Continue to focus your awareness on your breathing and the contraction and expansion it creates within your body.

Beneath your hands, imagine a liquid golden light, smooth, warm and shimmering at the core of your being.

This liquid golden light is your own inner light. Let yourself connect with the liquid light as it flows within you. With every breath your light gets stronger and brighter and becomes a living energy, a sensation that is palpable beneath your hands.

Now, in your mind's eye, imagine the sun, see the sun as living light and begin to drink the energy of this living light into every part of your being. Let the light enter from the crown of your head and draw it down beneath your hands. Let the light enter from the soles of your feet and draw it up to your core, gathering it beneath your hands.

Now let this living light be absorbed through the back of your body; the entire back of your body absorbs this light as it gathers at your centre beneath your hands. Now let the light enter the front of your body – the whole front of your body is suffused in this powerful golden light which gathers at your core. Let the light envelop your entire body, saturating every cell as the sun's living light and your own liquid light gather as one at the core of your being.

Take a deep breath, pulling your belly in as you do so, and on the exhale gently chant the sound 'Ram', letting the sound be made for the full length of your exhale.

Again, breathe in, contracting your belly, and on the exhale, chant the sound 'Ram', the sound for personal power and self-confidence.

Repeat for up to ten breaths, chanting this sound for your soul… Ram, Ram, Ram, Ram, Ram, Ram, Ram, Ram, Ram, Ram.

With your hands gently resting on your belly, sit quietly for a moment and notice the effect of the chant on your physical, emotional and spiritual body.

On your next inhale, receive divine light and, on the exhale, give out divine light.

Repeat for five breaths, giving and receiving divine light.

When you are ready, use your hands to place yourself in an energetic bubble of bright golden light to seal your meditation practice.

Affirmation: 'I am a being of radiant light.'

Path of the heart

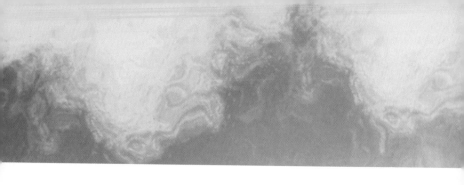

✳ Sit comfortably in a quiet place with your spine straight, but not stiff. Relax your jaw, tongue and throat. Relax your shoulders downwards and spread your collarbones apart.

Breathe deeply, knowing there is nowhere else to go and no one else you need to be other than yourself right here, right now, in this moment.

The path to your heart is through your breath, so if you find yourself holding your breath at any time, remember to use *Water Breathing* (see page 17), inhaling in through your nose and out through your mouth to reset your breathing and reconnect with yourself.

Take a moment to set your intention. If you would like one to use, then 'The whole of my heart is open' is good for today.

Inhale, contracting your belly, and on the exhale, chant the sound of 'Om'. Repeat three times and then, as the vibrations settle, place your right hand on your heart and your left hand on your belly.

As you inhale, draw your belly in and feel the cool air entering your nostrils. Pay attention to the breath as it travels up to the bridge of your nose and down through the back of your throat. Let the breath expand your throat. Inhale again whenever you need to and track the breath again into your nostrils and down into your throat, expanding your throat and following the breath as it moves into your chest cavity. As the lungs need to fill again, contract your belly by moving your navel towards your spine and track the air as it moves into your nostrils and down the back of your throat, feeling your throat expand and your chest filling, and feel the breath fill the area behind and around your heart.

On the next inhale, track the breath all the way to your heart and, as you do, connect with your outer heart – the part of your heart that interfaces with the world and also the threshold for accessing the rest of your heart. Pay attention to your outer heart. Keep breathing as you consider these questions:

How does your outer heart feel?
What affects your outer heart?
What would your outer heart like you to know?

Take a deep breath and use the breath to go beyond your outer heart and into your inner heart. Keep breathing as you consider these questions:

How does your inner heart feel?
What affects your inner heart?
What would your inner heart like you to know?

Then take another deep breath and let it guide you beyond your inner heart into your secret heart. There are no questions to ask, no words are needed here. Sit quietly with yourself as you fall into the vast expansiveness of your secret heart.

See what needs to be seen.
Feel what needs to be felt.

There's no need to explain it, make sense of it or fade it. Simply let it be and keep breathing as you come home to the place where you belong.

When you are ready to return to the here and now, bring your hands together in prayer at your heart centre and say your name silently to yourself. Bow your head in respect as you honour yourself right here, right now, and say, 'Namaste' to close the meditation.

Affirmation: 'I am pure and eternal love.'

Oxygen

Sit comfortably in a quiet place with your spine straight, but not stiff. Become aware of the contact you have with the ground beneath you. Notice how your weight is distributed, left and right, front and back, inside and outside. Shift your position slowly until you feel completely comfortable, even and balanced. Roll your shoulders back and down, and gently stretch open your collarbones. Tip your chin to your chest and either lower your gaze or close your eyes. Rest your hands in your lap, with the palms facing up.

Focus your attention on the natural rhythm of your breath and notice as your chest expands and your belly rises and falls.

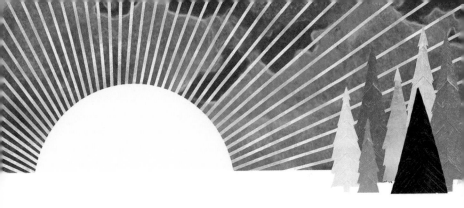

You're going to count your breath up to ten, preparing with a
nice, slow breath in through your nose and counting the next
exhale as breath number one. Like this:

Inhale slowly through your nose.

Exhale breath number one.
Inhale number one.

Exhale number two.
Inhale number two.

Exhale number three.
Inhale number three.

Exhale number four.
Inhale number four.

Exhale number five.
Inhale number five.

Exhale number six.
Inhale number six.

Exhale number seven.
Inhale number seven.

Exhale number eight.
Inhale number eight.

Exhale number nine.
Inhale number nine.

Exhale number ten.
Inhale number ten.

As you let go of the counting, you find yourself on a beautiful, unspoilt mountaintop, the sun's rosy rays promising hope and inviting you into a brand-new day. The mountain air is crisp and clean.

It is the freshest air you have ever tasted, and you drink in the pure air, breathing in life.

A light wind dances across your face and around your body. You can feel the wind is clearing your body and mind.

As fresh pure air enters your nostrils, your lungs expand and your mind becomes clearer and sharper. Everything feels still and it's as if the world opens before you as you look far out to the horizon and beyond. You allow your mind to expand with the expansiveness of the view. With every breath you feel more open and expansive.

As you open and expand, you become aware that you are the mountain, you are the sky, the trees, the breeze. There is peace deepening within you with every breath, inhaling and exhaling. With every breath, you see that there are no boundaries here, no limits.

Everything is one, as it is meant to be.

Everything is possible here. Your heart fills with joy, as your mind sees what is possible for you in your life at this time. Let the picture come in closer to you.

Bring the vision into clearer and sharper focus now. See what is possible. Open your heart and mind to what is possible. Expand your entire being into what is possible. Without boundaries, without limits, simply opening and expanding with every breath you take. Fuelled by the purity of the breath of life.

When you are ready, begin to bring your attention back to where you are now, feeling yourself rooted and grounded. Deeply present in your body. Feeling completely grounded and present in your body now. As you return to the here and now, opening your eyes and bringing yourself back into the room and this present moment. Say to yourself three times, 'I am right here, right now.'

Affirmation: 'My breath sustains me every day in every way.'

Desert bloom

✳ Sit comfortably in a quiet place with your spine straight, but not stiff. Close your eyes and start to become aware of your body. Becoming aware of the structure and form of your body, feeling the edges of you making contact with the seat beneath you. Becoming aware of the surface of your skin. Becoming aware of the surface of your skin containing the whole of your body, your skin holding the outer structure and form of your body. Become aware of your body within your skin, your muscles and your bones creating the structure and form of your inner body and holding your internal organs in place. Become aware of your blood moving around your body. Become aware of your heart beating, steadily, rhythmically. Every part of you connected. Become aware of your breathing, breath by breath by breath…

As you breathe, an opening is made in your mind. A place where your thoughts clear to reveal a place of serenity, an oasis of tranquillity. You find yourself walking effortlessly over soft sand towards this lush green oasis. The sun's rays are just beginning to creep over the horizon as a new day dawns, turning the sky from midnight blue to a soft delicate pink.

Picture the colours in your mind's eye as the sky shifts from pink, to purple, to red, then orange, yellow and gold.

As you get closer to the oasis, you see there are palm trees, cacti and vegetation here. Water comes from deep underground, sourcing life, creating and supporting this fertile area. You walk to the oasis and sit on a warm rock, next to a bubbling spring. From here, you notice movement between some other rocks. You look closely to see a snake in the final throes of shedding its skin. You watch mesmerized by the snake as it rubs against the rocks, until it is finally free and glides over to the spring to drink, leaving its old skin behind. Eventually, the snake has rested enough, and it continues on its way.

You begin to wonder what you might need to shed in your life. What would you like to let go of at this time? What might be holding you back, or keeping you stuck? You let these thoughts come to your mind. Becoming aware of what you can safely let go of at this time. When you are ready to let go, you slide off your rock into the crystal-clear, blue water of the spring. Taking a deep breath, you submerge yourself under the water, cleansing and purifying your entire being, letting go easily, without challenge or difficulty. You feel refreshed and energized, and return to your rock, to absorb how you feel after letting go.

This is a moment just for you.

So you let go and allow yourself to rest and relax deeply in this moment, letting go right here, right now. Feeling calm and relaxed as you let go. Resting deeply. Letting go. The oasis has sourced you in the same way it sources the lush, fertile vegetation around it. You feel grateful to know that you can return to this source at any time, but you know that it is now time to leave.

You retrace your steps with ease. Become more aware of your breath with every step. Letting your breathing bring you back, inhaling fully and exhaling fully. Becoming aware of the edges of you making contact with the seat beneath you, as you open your eyes and take a moment to adjust to being back in the here and now.

Affirmation: 'I let go with ease and grace.'

Crystal mountain

✳ For this meditation, lie flat on your back, with your arms by your sides and your palms facing up. Take three deep breaths, inhaling through your nose and out through your mouth. Let go of any tension in your body. Let go of any worries that may have arisen as you start your day. Focus on your breathing, allowing your body to be relaxed. With each breath your body and mind become more and more relaxed.

Follow the flow of your breath.

As you breathe, you imagine the sound of the wind outside. The wind is calling your name, inviting you on a journey to the crystal mountain. You feel the wind coming closer, whispering the sound of your name with every breath you take.

You follow the wind and the sound of your name, which guide you toward the start of a pure white crystal path that is leading you to a mountain glowing blue in the distance. See yourself standing on this crystal path – it is quiet, with the sun's delicate rays illuminating the way.

You start walking along this crystal path with the wind for company. Along the way, you see a beautiful valley. You pause for a moment, observing nature in all her beauty. You hear the sound of waterfalls running through the valley and watch the sun rise crimson into the sky, absorbing the sun's energy into your whole being. You continue to walk, getting higher and closer to the mountain which glows with a soft blue light.

The sparkling crystal mountain is now directly in front of you. The mountain is formed of a magnificent blue crystal, which is embedded deep in the earth and rises high into the sky. Purple amethysts surround the base of the mountain, flashing and sparkling in the sunlight, and you look down to see the white crystal path has changed, and you are now standing on a path of deep red rubies. You feel a current of energy pouring in through the soles of your feet, up through your legs, your knees, your thighs, the base of your spine.

The wind gently blows back in, gently placing a large, yellow citrine crystal in your hands, and you hold the crystal at the centre of your body above your navel. The citrine has come from the centre of the blue crystal mountain.

From the core of the mountain to the core of you, the energy is connected.

You feel it pulsating through your entire body in gentle waves. The citrine balances and clears you, and you feel energized.

The path leads you into a tunnel, which reaches deep inside the crystal mountain. The walls inside the mountain are entirely embedded with jade, malachite and emeralds. You raise your arms towards the walls and the energy pours in through your palms.

The tunnel continues to a crystal room within the heart of the mountain. In this room, the walls are studded with diamonds so bright it is almost dazzling. At the centre of the crystal room is a formation of rose quartz. You kneel before the formation and open your heart to the healing power of rose quartz.

When you are ready to leave, you continue through the tunnel and the wind calls your name, guiding you back down the other side of the mountain along a pure white crystal path. Your aura shines brightly with every step you take.

You let your light shine, emanating pure love into the world.

As you return to the beginning of the path, the wind carries you gently to the place where you were lying. You become aware of your physical body, as you slowly open your eyes, with the image of the crystal mountain imprinted into your mind, your heart and your entire being.

Affirmation: 'I am energized and recharged.'

Soaring

✳ In your own time, find a comfortable position for your body. Begin by closing your eyes. Inhaling and exhaling. Inhaling calm, exhaling stress. When your mind wanders, simply focus on your breathing. Inhaling and exhaling. Your breath soothes and eases you. Inhaling calm, exhaling stress.

When you are ready, imagine that you are standing on a clifftop, somewhere beautiful in nature. You are looking over the ocean, and, with every inhale, you fill your lungs with refreshing sea air. In the distance, you hear birds flying, their wings beating rhythmically and sounding like a steady heartbeat.

With the next breath, your whole body lets go – it is as if you are flying like a bird. You spread your wings, step off the edge of the cliff and immediately feel a sensation at your core, as you are uplifted on a thermal. Drifting freely among white clouds in the blue sky. The warm air pushes against your wings and you feel yourself spreading your wings, experiencing how easy and enjoyable it is to feel light and free. Every beat of your wings feels like freedom.

You feel alive, energized and free.

You soar over endless ocean and above the clouds now, enjoying your vision from high above, a place where you are utterly free and have access to higher perspective.

Higher vision.

Higher perspective.

From this vantage point, all that you need to know can be seen. You use this feeling of distance to gain a new perspective on something that may be of interest or concern to you. Perhaps it's something that makes you happy which is worth appreciating. Or an issue that you want to resolve.

You quietly contemplate this in the privacy of your own thoughts, letting the wisdom you need in this moment in time be received.

From this vantage point, you have complete clarity and know all is well.

When you are ready to return, you glide slowly and effortlessly back to the clifftop.

Take notice of your breathing and allow your breath to bring you back. Take notice of your body as you return fully and consciously to the physical space you are in. Allow yourself to awaken and return.

Open your eyes and stretch your arms, remembering that these are your wings, and you can fly freely at any time.

Affirmation: 'I am free.'

Seeds of intention

✳ Sit or lie in a quiet place where you can relax. Close your eyes and breathe quietly and slowly in and out through your nose. Take a moment to settle and focus your attention on your breath. Noticing the sensation of breath in this moment. As you breathe, you know that relaxation is normal and natural, and your body will do this on its own. You can help your body relax right now by setting an intention to feel the most relaxed you have all day.

With every breath you take, you feel more and more relaxed.

If thoughts about your day ahead arise, just let them be. You don't need to do anything with them in this moment – you are letting thought just come and go.

Now bring awareness to your right hand.
Notice each finger of your right hand.

Touch your right thumb to index finger… thumb to middle
finger… thumb to fourth finger… thumb to little finger…
thumb to fourth finger… thumb to middle finger… thumb
to index finger.

Relax your hand. Relax your fingers.

Notice your left hand.
Notice each finger of your left hand.

Touch your left thumb to index finger… thumb to middle
finger… thumb to fourth finger… thumb to little finger…
thumb to fourth finger… thumb to middle finger… thumb
to index finger.

Relax your hand. Relax your fingers.

Now you are going to focus your attention on letting an intention arise. You will do this by asking yourself a question. Don't try hard here. Stay soft and relaxed. If at any time you find you are holding your breath, exhale fully so that your breathing naturally resets. Ask yourself:

Physically, for the benefit of my health and well-being, in one word what do I need?

Notice what comes up for you.

Emotionally, for the benefit of my heart, in one word what do I need?

Notice what comes up for you.

Spiritually, for the benefit of my soul journey, what do I need?

Notice what comes up for you.

Now imagine you are holding these three words as seeds of intention in the palm of your right hand.

Place your right hand on your forehead and plant the seeds of intention in your mind.

Place your right hand over your heart space and plant the seeds of your intention in your heart.

Place your right hand on your belly, above your navel, and place your left hand on top of your right. Plant the seeds of your intention deep in your core.

Affirmation: 'I am open to receive the goodness of life.'

Dance your
dreams alive

✳ An old woman sits on a hand-knotted rug, weaving baskets from water reeds in the corner of a dusty market square. As you enter the square, you realize the place is unfamiliar to you. You know that you are entering unknown realms, but you feel safe, still and at ease within. The floor is uneven underfoot and a pale pink, microscopic dust rests lightly on the ground. You look behind and see your footprints imprinted in the dust.

As you approach, the woman looks up from her weaving and smiles kindly. Her eyes are mesmerizing, deep pools of wisdom. 'Welcome, you have arrived here, at this moment in time, as the weavers expected you would. You are here to weave your destiny. You can sit with me here,' she says, patting the small cushion on the rug next to her. You sit down, noticing your footprints and the path that has led you here.

As you sit quietly with the weaver woman, you begin to notice the movement of breath through your nostrils and you follow that movement into your body.

With each breath, you begin to feel the rise and fall of your chest and the expansion and softening in your belly. You become even more aware of your breath now.

You notice where you feel the breath the most clearly in your body and anchor your mind in that spot.

The weaver woman is wrapped in soft saffron silks, bleached over lifetimes by the everlasting sun. She passes you a basket of water reeds, and you begin to weave your own basket. You know exactly what to do, threading and weaving the reeds, breathing deep and full, breathing long and slow.

As you weave, the woman begins to speak. She tells you:

'As you weave, you are openly dreaming of all that you want for your life. These dreams are yet to be dreams. It is time to open your heart to what is yet to be, as you weave every step of your destiny.'

Your heart melts and your mind softens as you begin to drift into a delicious daydream.

You ask yourself: 'What kind of future do I feel deeply moved towards?'

With every breath, you let your imagination wander as it dances its way into a positive future that you feel deeply moved towards.

In your mind's eye:

See yourself in that future.
See others in that future.
See what inspires you in that future.
See who and what you love in that future.
See what grounds you in that future.
See what you are called for in that future.
See your place called home in that future.
See the planet in that future.

Hold yourself in the highest positive regard in that future.

Breathe…

Hold others in the highest positive regard in that future.

Breathe…

Hold the planet in the highest positive regard in that future.

Breathe…

In just a moment, you are going to return to the place you came from. Gently counting back to the square where you were weaving: 3, 2, 1. You are sitting next to the weaver woman again. It is time to go now. You bow in respect to her, and then begin to retrace your steps in the pink, microscopic dust, knowing deep down that where you have come from will lead you to where you are going.

All is well.

Bring your hands together in prayer at your heart centre
and bow to yourself, because you are the weaver of your
own destiny. When you are ready, open your eyes and come
back to the room.

Affirmation: 'I am creating a positive future.'

Finding the flow

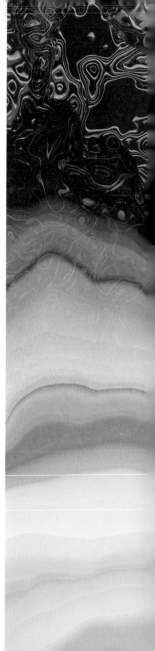

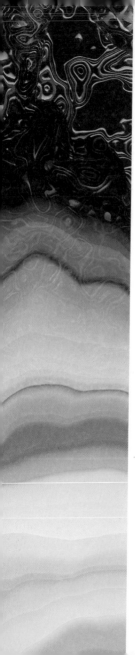

Sit comfortably in a quiet place with your spine straight, but not stiff. For this meditation it's recommended that you hold a crystal in the palm of each hand. Tiger's-eye is particularly good for balance and encouragement. If you don't own any crystals, then simply imagine holding them in your hands instead.

Place one of the tiger's-eye crystals in each palm. Rest your palms on your knees and let your hands relax.

Feel the energy of the crystal in your left hand. The texture, weight, temperature. Connect your energy with the energy of the crystal and amplify the energy of the crystal. Breathing in and breathing out.

Now feel the energy of the crystal in your right hand. The texture, weight, temperature. Connect your energy with the energy of the crystal and amplify the energy of the crystal. Breathing in and breathing out.

Arc the energy from your right palm to your left. With the next inhale, draw the energy up your left arm, into your shoulder. Exhale, and on the next inhale draw the energy to the left side of your face, and then arc the energy into the right hemisphere of your brain. Looping it back, arc the energy over to the left side of your brain and send it down your left arm into your left hand, feeling the weight of the crystal in your left palm, as the energy moves into the left side of your body.

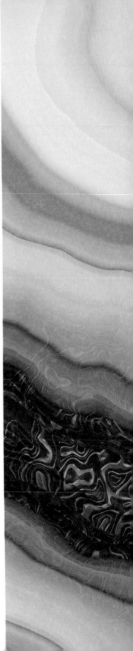

Finding the flow

Remember to breathe as the energy goes down the left side of your body. Left outer thigh. Left shin. Outside of the left foot to your little toe, and then arcing the energy over to your right foot. Little toe of your right foot, outside of the right foot.

Feel the energy on the outer right shin, on the outside of your right thigh, your whole right side. Move the energy into your right palm, feeling the crystal in your palm as the energy moves up your right arm to your right shoulder and then, with the next breath, inhale into the right side of your face, sending the energy to the left hemisphere of your brain.

Looping it back, arc the energy over to the right side of your brain and send it back down your right arm into your right palm and then into the right side of your body.

Remember to breathe as the energy goes down the right side of your body. Right outer thigh. Right shin. Outside of the right foot to your little toe, and then arcing the energy over to your left foot. Little toe of your left foot, outside of the left foot. Feel the energy on the outer left shin, on the outside of your left thigh, your whole left side. Move the energy into your left palm, feeling the crystal in your palm.

Take a breath and feel the weight of the crystal in each hand.

Connect with the energy of the crystal in each hand and arc the energy from left palm to right and back again. Repeating several times, letting the energy flow from left to right, right to left.

Now place your right hand in your left hand and bring both hands to your power centre, just above your belly button. Hold your hands here.

Let the energy flow deep into your core.

When you are ready, take a breath, lower your hands and open your eyes. You may wish to sit quietly with your eyes open for a few minutes as you complete this meditation.

Affirmation: 'I am balanced.'

Through the eye
of the telescope

✳ Sit comfortably in a quiet place with your spine straight, but not stiff. You are going to begin this meditation with some eye movements. These movements are done slowly, without straining and with your eyes closed. The directions in which you move your eyes will follow the points of a compass, the four main points plus the points in between: upper left, upper right, lateral left, lateral right, lower left, lower right, straight down, straight up.

The following instructions are for you if you are right-handed. If you are left-handed, reverse the instructions and start with upper right, upper left and so on, before finishing with straight down, straight up.

Keep your eyes gently closed throughout the meditation.

Contract your belly, bringing the navel gently towards your spine as you inhale through the nostrils. As you inhale, slowly begin to move the eyes from the centre, without straining, toward the first direction, upper left. Release the eyes as you exhale, allowing them to return to centre.

Contract your belly, bringing the navel towards your spine as you inhale through the nostrils, and, as you inhale, repeat the sequence in the second direction, upper right, nice and slowly, without straining. Release the eyes as you exhale, allowing them to return to centre.

Contract your belly, bringing the navel towards your spine as you inhale through the nostrils. As you inhale, begin to move the eyes from the centre slowly, without straining, toward the next direction, lateral left. Release the eyes as you exhale, allowing them to return to centre.

Contract your belly, bringing the navel towards your spine as you inhale through the nostrils. As you inhale, begin to move the eyes from the centre slowly, without straining, toward the next direction, lateral right. Release the eyes as you exhale, allowing them to return to centre.

Contract your belly, bringing the navel towards your spine as you inhale through the nostrils. As you inhale, begin to move the eyes from the centre slowly, without straining, toward the next direction, lower left. Release the eyes as you exhale, allowing them to return to centre.

Contract your belly, bringing the navel towards your spine as you inhale through the nostrils. As you inhale, begin to move the eyes from the centre slowly, without straining, toward the next direction, lower right. Release the eyes as you exhale, allowing them to return to centre.

Contract your belly, bringing the navel towards your spine as you inhale through the nostrils. As you inhale, begin to move the eyes from the centre slowly, without straining, straight down. Release the eyes as you exhale, allowing them to return to centre.

Finally, contract your belly, bringing the navel towards your spine as you inhale through the nostrils. As you inhale, begin to move the eyes from the centre slowly, without straining, straight up.

Release the eyes as you exhale, allowing them to return to centre.

Release all eye movements now, and completely relax, letting the tiny muscles around your eyes relax. The muscles in your forehead relax. Your face muscles relax. Relaxing your jaw and throat now. As you breathe naturally, imagine that you have your eye to a telescope.

You are looking into the sky and space beyond using a telescope.

As you look through the telescope, you become aware of something in your line of sight that has been bothering you for a while. Something that has been challenging, or frustrating.

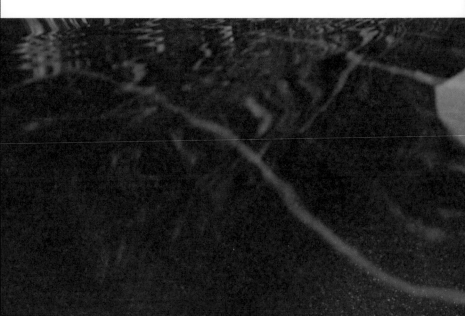

Something that you have struggled to resolve or know what to do about, You bring the problem into close focus so that you see it more clearly, and then you zoom out on the problem so that you can get a different perspective. You ask your higher self what would help you to resolve this problem right now and pay close attention to the guidance you receive.

When you are ready, you bring your focus back to the here and now. Feel yourself grounded and rooted in your seat, rub your hands rigorously up and down your arms, and then open your eyes.

Affirmation: 'I trust in the power of my free will.'

* Weekend meditations

The meditations

At the weekend, take some time to start your day slowly, luxuriously even, with a longer morning meditation. These meditations are designed to take you on a guided journey into deeper realms, so allow yourself 15 or 20 minutes to really sink into the experience.

As always, create a space where you can feel completely comfortable. Choose your favourite easy chair or a comfy cushion, light a candle or some incense. You could begin your meditation by preparing some tea and sitting quietly, savouring it for a few minutes. If you are sitting on a cushion, cross your legs; if you are sitting in a chair, place both feet flat on the floor. If you like to use crystals, you can bring them into your meditation space or hold them in your hands. Stay warm with socks and a blanket if needed. If there are other people at home with you, let them know you're going to have some undisturbed quiet time.

When you are ready, sit in a comfortable position with your spine straight, but not stiff. Rest your hands in your lap or on your knees. Begin by inhaling deeply and exhaling slowly three times and take a moment to set a positive intention for yourself during this morning's meditation. Lower your gaze and tip your chin to your chest, turning your attention inwards as you gently bring your eyelids together and focus on your breath entering and leaving your body.

The tree of life

✳ Sit comfortably in a quiet place with your spine straight, but not stiff. Start by taking three nice, big, deep breaths, breathing in and breathing out. With the next out-breath, gently close your eyes and start to feel the weight of your body making contact with the surface beneath you. Let your hands relax, and if you notice any sounds, bring your mind back and gently settle into your seat.

Imagine you are in a rainforest, swinging in a hammock. Gently drifting off. Feeling completely relaxed and at ease. All around you the sounds of life are ever-present. You allow these sounds to fade away into the distance, letting your attention drift towards nothing in particular.

Nowhere to go, nowhere to be, other than in this moment, right here, right now.

You are awakened by the rhythm of the falling rain and you surrender to the moment, letting the rain wash away any pain or suffering you have felt, either recently or in the past. You let every drop of rain cleanse your pain away.

As your pain washes away, you feel open and expansive. It is as though you can feel the spirits in the trees, rocks and plants. You begin to hear the spirits calling you, inviting you on a journey, and you leave your hammock and before you a path starts to form.

The path leads you deeper into the rainforest, and with every step you take, you feel your senses sharpening. You can see clearly, hear clearly, feel clearly. You pause, absorbing the beauty of nature all around you. Every shade of green dazzles and dances around you.

It is a healthy, happy place to be, surrounded by nature, and you feel uplifted.

Ahead of you the trees start to thin, and you notice a clearing. A place where the light is even brighter, a place that radiates peace and calm. At the centre of the clearing is a very large tree. You walk towards the tree, its energy drawing you in like a hypnotic force.

The tree is sacred, ancient and wise, with deep roots spreading far beneath the earth, connecting to all life in the underworld. A majestic trunk that curves in the middle supports branches as they reach out and connect to all life beyond them in the middle world. At the very top of the tree its crown reaches upwards, connecting to all life in the heavenly realms.

You step towards the tree and place your hands on its trunk. You feel an instant connection as the energy from the tree awakens within you. You breathe and let a question form in your mind. When you are ready, you ask the tree your question. Breathing steadily, waiting for the response. In time, you hear the answer and place your cheek on the tree trunk in gratitude, before turning and sitting at the base of the tree.

Here you stay quietly absorbing the answer the tree gave you.

As you sit at the base of the tree, you feel the interconnectedness of life.

You feel that you are a part of it. The energy comes up from the earth, is channelled through you, up through the trunk and out to the tips of the branches, returning to earth and then back up through you and the trunk into the heavens – and so it is. A continuous cycle of energy that sources all life.

On the next breath, become aware of your body making contact with the surface beneath you. Scrunch your toes and release them. Tense and release the muscles in your legs. Bring your shoulders up to your ears and then gently exhale as you release them. Rotate your chin in a semi-circle in front of your body, from the right shoulder to your left and back again. Stretch your arms to the sky and, when you are ready, open your eyes and return to the room.

Affirmation:

'In my soul I have roots like a tree.
In my soul I have peace like a mountain.
In my soul I have love like an ocean.
In my soul I have joy like a river.'

Sands of time

✳ Breathe deeply three times. With each breath, let yourself travel all the way down to the deepest, most welcome place of calm and relaxation within you.

For this meditation, you invite your spirit guide to be alongside you on the journey. Trust however they show up for you. A power animal, an angel or an ancestral elder.

You feel their presence and know that you will be supported and guided along the way.

You are going to go back in time, to honour your lineage. Some of the people you meet you will remember and recall; others you won't, but they are still a part of the line that led you to be here.

To begin, in your mind's eye, visualize an hourglass. The sand slowly runs through, grain by grain. You focus your attention on these grains of sand as they flow in a fine stream, grain by grain. Each grain is individual, but forms part of the whole.

As the sand continues to flow, you realize that the sands of time never run out.

It is a continuous flow for all time. Each grain represents a person who has existed on this planet. Everyone an individual. Everyone a part of the whole.

You take this moment to reflect on you and who you are, and where you are. What makes you who you are? What led you to where you are? You realize that your story and your experiences are shaped by those who came before you. The good and the bad woven together by the fabric of your ancestors.

Begin to visualize your family line, your parents, starting first with your mother and then your father. As you see your parents, you ask your spirit guide, 'What wisdom do my parents have for me?' You receive the wisdom with gratitude.

You continue to move through your family line, asking your spirit guide to convey the wisdom from each person and receiving this wisdom with gratitude. You go to the end of your family line as you know it. Receiving wisdom with gratitude. As you reach the end of the family line as you know it, your spirit guide looks deeper into the ancestral line on your behalf. Your spirit guide has a message from your ancestors which they want to share with you. You receive the message with an open heart and deep gratitude. You ask your spirit guide to send a message to all of those who came before that you do not remember.

Your message is: 'I love and respect the light that shines within you.'

Your spirit guide tells you that the ancestors send blessings of love back to you.

You feel grateful to be a part of this story, woven by your ancestors, continued by your current family line, a beautifully imperfect tapestry stretching into an as yet unknown future.

You thank your spirit guide for making this journey with you, as you breathe deeply three times. With each breath, let yourself travel all the way down to the deepest, most welcome place of calm and relaxation within you. When you are ready, scrunch and release your toes, tense and release the muscles in your legs. Stretch your arms above your head, let out an audible sigh and then, in your own time, open your eyes.

Affirmation: 'I honour the story of my past.'

Soul star

✳ Sit comfortably in a quiet place with your spine straight, but not stiff. Begin your journey by closing your eyes. Become aware of the energy at the base of your spine. As you breathe, feel the energy moving up and down your spine. With each in-breath the energy rises up your spine to the crown of your head; with each out-breath the energy descends from the crown of your head to the base of your spine. Now breathe up the whole of your body, from the soles of your feet, up through your spine and up to the crown of your head, and then back down. Do this ten times.

Breathing in – energy flows up from the soles of your feet.

Breathing out – energy flows down from the crown of your head.

Becoming deeply relaxed.

Letting your mind rest in calmness.

Now extend your focus from the soles of your feet to the core of the earth.

Breathing in, the energy rises up from the core of the earth.

Breathing out, the energy flows back to the earth.

Feeling more and more relaxed with every breath you take.

Now extend your focus to the universe of stars above you. Bright white points of light suspended in the expansiveness of space.

Breathing in from the universe of stars into the crown of your head and out through the soles of your feet.

Breathing in from the core of the earth, up into the universe of stars, and breathing the energy back in through the crown of your head.

Now that you have made contact with the stars in the expansiveness of space, one star in particular stands out to you.

This is a special star to you, because it is your soul star.

Put your focus on your soul star. Anchor there.

Breathing in – energy flows up from the earth's core.

Breathing out – energy flows down from the soul star.

Repeat ten times.

This is the place you have come from and the place that you will return to. Deep down you know the truth: that you are part of the cosmos. Connected to and part of the infinite rhythms of the cosmos. You know that you belong. You know that you are whole.

You continue to connect with your soul star, and your soul star connects with you.

Your soul star speaks, transmitting this message to every cell in your being:

The wisdom that flows through the whole of the universe also flows through you.

The truth that flows through the whole of the universe also flows through you.

The love that flows through the whole of the universe also flows through you.

The energy that flows through the whole of the universe also flows through you.

Breathing in – energy flows up from the earth's core.
Breathing out – energy flows down from the soul star.

Every cell in your body feels attuned and aligned.

When you are ready, breathe up the whole of your body, from the soles of your feet, up through your spine and up to the crown of your head, and then back down.

Now become aware of the energy at the base of your spine. As you breathe, feel the energy moving up and down your spine. With each in-breath the energy rises up your spine to the crown

of your head; with each out-breath the energy descends from the crown of your head to the base of your spine. Begin to bring your focus to your belly as you inhale and exhale, feeling your belly rise and fall. Letting your breath return to its normal rhythm now, nice and easy.

Coming back into yourself, coming back into the here and now. Feeling your body making contact with the seat beneath you. The edges of you making contact with the seat beneath you. Breathing nice and easy, as you begin to open your eyes gently and return to the room.

Affirmation: 'I am connected to the infinite universe.'

Into the deep ocean

✳ You are going on a journey into the unknown. Your journey begins with you swimming in a vast, calm ocean which stretches to the horizon in every direction. Your breathing is relaxed and easy with every stroke you make. Inhaling and exhaling, smoothly and fully.

The water is pleasantly calm and cool, and you can smell the salt in the air.

Breath by breath, you feel relaxed and calm. Although you are swimming, you don't feel overexerted. It is a gentle, restful swim. Stroke by stroke, breath by breath.

You focus your attention on your breathing. Noticing your breath with every stroke. Is it long or short? Deep or shallow? If it is short or shallow, take some small sips of air, filling the tops of your lungs little by little. Now take a deep inhale and, on the exhale, fully release the air from the whole of your lungs: the top lung, the middle lung and the lower lung.

As time passes, you see an object in the ocean. You swim towards it with a sense of curiosity, and as it gets closer, you see it is a wooden raft. You pull yourself up onto the raft and enjoy a welcome rest. The sun's rays gently warm your body and you relax even more, feeling completely rested as you bask in the sun, with the waves gently rocking beneath you.

When you are ready, you climb off the raft and immerse your whole body in the cool water.

Feeling completely relaxed, you begin to go deeper into the water.

Allowing yourself to sink deeper and deeper, letting go as you allow yourself to descend to the depths, sinking deeper and deeper. Down towards the songs of the whales.

You feel totally at ease and safe, and in the distance, you hear a whale call. The call is the sound of your name echoing through the vast depths of the ocean, heard for miles around.

Your name blends with the sound of the whale song, and you know you are welcome here.

Out of the deep blue, a whale glides towards you, its huge head drifts by and you can look deeply into its eyes. As you connect with this magnificent creature, you enjoy the special encounter. As you look deeply into the whale's gentle eyes, it looks back at you. It has seen so much and is the keeper of stories over time. You ask yourself, what might the whale see in me? What story would it sing for me?

After some time, the whale blinks and then begins to dive down into the inky black ocean depths. As it leaves, you hear the whale's song blending with your name. You begin to swim upwards, using strong strokes towards the sun dancing on the surface of the ocean. As you break through the surface, your raft is waiting for you and you climb back on.

A gentle breeze begins to blow your raft back to the shore, as you focus on your breath, inhaling and exhaling, smoothly and fully. Breath by breath, you begin to bring yourself back to the here and now. Feeling refreshed and relaxed, you feel fully seen by the encounter you had with the whale and know you can let yourself be seen by others in the world.

Affirmation: 'I am fully seen.'

*The seasons

Spring

✳ On a beautiful spring morning, you step outside for a walk in the countryside, setting your intention as you take your first steps on the path. For miles around you can see fields of golden daffodils nodding in the breeze, dotted on the horizon with green woodlands. The path you take through the countryside is quiet and you are undisturbed, apart from a large, brown hare with long, black-tipped ears that sits looking at you quizzically.

The hare turns and begins to bound ahead along the path, its white tail inviting you to follow. With every step you take along the path, bright yellow daffodils set your heart alight with their blinding beauty, and you feel full of joy as you walk towards the woodland.

The hare guides you into the woodland where trees huddle together to create a protective canopy. As you enter the woodland, you notice the air is cooler and fresher here, where the rays of the sun are not able to penetrate easily.

It is a sanctuary of peace and tranquillity.

A sweet, earthy smell envelops you as you watch the hare dart between moss-covered tree stumps, moving easily around patches of ferns thriving in the protection of the cool, damp woodland.

At the base of the trees, purple crocuses with golden stamens have peeked through the earth, the trees providing them with their perfect shady home, and they remind you that spring is here. Tiny droplets of moisture rest on your cheeks and you pause to raise your face skywards, opening your throat and then taking a deep breath of pure, clean, fresh air.

As you inhale the fresh, woody aroma, you smell the distinctive, sweet and spicy scent of pine trees. Step by step, slowly walking deep into the woodland following the brown hare, your feet walk over a carpet of fallen pine needles. You enjoy the sensations of soaking up the healing powers of the woodland and the scent of pine, breathing the goodness of being here in this moment deeply into your whole being.

Summer

✳ You are standing on a rock, looking out to sea. The view is spectacular, and you place your right hand on your heart and breathe in deeply. Every wave that breaks beneath you is in time with the rhythm of your heart. You feel it beating gently in your chest, a steady, regular rhythm pumping the blood around your body with every beat.

The ocean moves in and out in time with your own heartbeat.

The morning sun sparkles in a clear blue sky, and shimmers over the bright blue ocean. You feel happy and content as you turn your face toward the light, then you turn your throat to the light and then you turn your heart to the light. Letting the light of the sun be absorbed by your heart as the rhythm of the ocean moves in time with the beat of your heart.

As you feel the sun on your face, you become aware of the tide within you. A subtle movement of energy that flows from your head, down your spine, and sends a life force running through your veins. This gentle, rhythmic tide is as essential to you as breathing. It is as though you have another way of breathing, a gentle breath of life that flows through your veins. This tide is connected to the ocean tide. As each wave breaks upon the shore, in time with your own heartbeat, the subtle breath of life flows through your veins, the same life force that rocks the ocean ebbs and flows around your body. You feel a part of it, and it is a part of you. You breathe in the wholeness and the completeness of this moment, right here, right now.

You feel this truth deep at the core of your being: All is one. All is well.

You place your right hand on your heart and listen as your heart shares a pure truth with you. Communicating a message that is just for you, right here, right now. You spend some time breathing in your truth and, as you get ready to leave, you place yourself in an azure blue bubble of light, blue like the colour of the ocean, blue like the sky on a clear day.

Autumn

✳ Morning mists hover lightly above the river, the air feels cool and slightly damp, and you walk along the path. The sunrise gently breaks the sky, turning it delicate shades of pink and gold. Slowly the leaves are loosening their grip, and, as they begin to fall, their amber hues come to a peaceful resting place before returning to the earth from which they came.

Your body relaxes with every breath you take. Your thoughts loosen, your body loosens, softening your face, softening your jaw, as you soften the tiny muscles around your eyes now. Softening your throat, letting your shoulders be soft now, softening your chest and, as you take a deep breath in, softening the space around your heart. Another breath as you relax at the core of you. Softening your stomach, your thighs, letting your knees soften, your calves soften, as your feet gently soften and your whole body relaxes now.

As your body softens and your mind softens, you become aware of a sound in the distance. The sound is the steady beat of wings as geese fly in formation through over the river. As each bird flaps its wings, it creates an uplift for the bird following behind. The geese instinctively know that they can fly further if they fly together. Each bird supports the others and this support creates a collective energy. When the bird at the front feels tired, it returns to the back of the formation to rest. The birds at the back send encouraging honks to support those at the front.

You think of your own support network. Calling into your mind's eye the people who are encouraging you along the way. Those who love and care for you, those who have your best interests at heart, those who want more than anything for you to be happy and succeed. You feel gratitude that you are supported, and you pause to acknowledge that there are times when you need to lead and times when you need to rest. You take a moment to check in with yourself to see what is needed in your life right now. Is it a time to lead or a time to rest?

As you listen to your truth, you hear the geese continuing their flight, as the sound of honking begins to fade into the distance. You become aware of breathing a perfect cycle of nature, just as the leaves return to the earth each autumn. Everything perfectly as it is meant to be. As you inhale, you notice the final wisps of mist dissolving as the sun warms the air. You feel ready to begin your day, knowing that if you need support you only have to honk…

Winter

✳ Moonlight casts a silver glow over a crisp fresh frost, which was laid down overnight and gently sprinkles the tree branches with a magical, glittering stardust. In this space before daybreak, everything is still. Everything is quiet – even the owl has finished hooting for the night and gently tucks its head under its wing.

From your window you watch as a fox quietly creeps back to its den, with the moon reflected in its eyes. The fox stops, sensing that it is being watched, and then turns around, making eye contact with you. Through the fox's eyes you have a window into your own soul, a way to see yourself more clearly than ever before. You see the goodness within you. The kindness within you, and, as you see yourself more clearly, you begin to connect to the compassion within you. Feeling the gratitude within you. You feel the love you have to offer to yourself and to others and to the world. In this moment, your heart opens and expands, love radiates through you and around you, and you are reminded that love is timeless. Love is eternal.